# Dream Incubation for Greater Self-Awareness

*a handbook*

Kelly Lydick, M.A.

Pure Carbon Publishing

ISBN 13: 978-0-9676887-7-0
EISBN: 978-0-9676887-8-7

LCCN: 2021951772

Edited by The Story Laboratory
www.writeeditdesignlab.com
Cover and interior design by Tabitha Lahr

For press inquiries, please contact the publisher at:
publicity@purecarbonpublishing.com

Printed in the United States of America
Second edition 2022

Published by Pure Carbon Publishing
An Imprint of Living Your Dream, LLC
PO Box 12342
Glendale, AZ 85318
www.purecarbonpublishing.com

## Praise for *Dream Incubation for Greater Self-Awareness*

"Many writers have described the process of dream incubation but nobody has done as thorough a job as Kelly Lydick in this remarkable book. She has provided a step-by-step procedure for programming dreams so that they respond to readers' hopes and goals, using intention as the key to obtaining answers to their questions, as well as remembering and implementing them. Lydick's reader-friendly instructions provide a road map for those readers who suspected that their dreams were of value but who never knew quite how to harvest their insights."

—Stanley Krippner, Ph.D., co-editor, *Working with Dreams and PTSD Nightmares*

"It's been said that all life is a dream. I don't know if that is exactly true, but I do know that our dreams can powerfully impact our life. The secret is understanding what they are trying to tell us . . . and also understanding how to program them for expanded insight about your life. In Kelly Lydick's book *Dream Incubation for Greater Awareness* she takes you, step-by-step, though a process to program (incubate) your dreams for higher awareness. You can feel her passion for the dreamtime in her book. May this book ignite your passion as well!"

—Denise Linn, author of *The Hidden Power of Dreams*, Gateway Dreaming and Soul Coaching Founder

*For those who choose to look inside and find their greatest path to growth: Transformative work is not for the faint of heart, but for the brave, for the courageous, for those who have the forethought to understand the rippling effect their internal actions have on the outer world. May you look to your dreams to guide your waking life.*

"... When an inner situation is not made conscious,
it happens outside, as fate."

—Carl Gustav Jung

# Contents

# Introduction

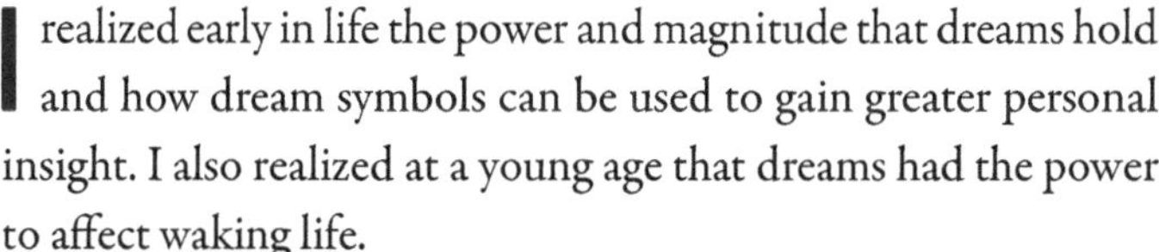

I realized early in life the power and magnitude that dreams hold and how dream symbols can be used to gain greater personal insight. I also realized at a young age that dreams had the power to affect waking life.

The world of dreams is vast and mysterious, intriguing, and full of wonder. It holds the potential for great personal insights, for new information about the self and the world to be learned, and even to be able to enter into other realms and gain insight about life itself.

I've been journaling my dreams since I was a teen. I see them as information and as mythical stories, set about to help us each learn and grow in a way that's exciting and exhilarating, and profound—if we're willing to pay attention. I've seen dreams give birth to new creative projects, offer answers to health issues and ailments, provide insight into areas that seem to be stuck, offer solutions to ordinary problems, and more. The power of dreams can be profound if you choose to engage with this world.

It's my hope that this book will help give you the beginnings of a solid Dream Incubation practice and will also allow you to appreciate the power that dreams can hold.

In this book you'll learn a brief history of dreaming practices from different cultures around the world, and you'll learn about the biology of dreams. You'll learn how to use the Dream Incubation process, and you'll learn how to use a dream journal to increase your dreaming effectiveness.

You'll also learn how to frame questions that yield rapid results with the Incubation process, and I'll give you tips for maximum results that you can use on your own when you start your own dreaming practice. At the end of each chapter, there will be a journaling or research activity exercise for you to complete. For this chapter, begin by journaling about the following questions and see what is revealed to you.

### *Pre-Dream Incubation Inventory*

1. Do you usually dream in color or black and white?
2. How often to you remember your dreams, on average?
3. What are your goals with the Dream Incubation process?
4. What areas of your life would you like to improve?

## *Chapter 1:*

# The Power of Dream Incubation

Dream Incubation is a process that has been used by cultures worldwide for thousands of years. Native Americans, the Greeks, the Egyptians, and others, all revered dreams and the process of engaging with dream content as a way of being part of the greater reality of life. These cultures held in high regard the information that came from dreams, and used that information to inform their choices about the waking life.

What ancients knew then, we are now able to use in a more modern and updated way that still works well with modern life. Psychologists have since studied the Dream Incubation Technique and have documented in clinical studies the validity of this technique (Delaney, 1976).

Dream Incubation, in part, is a process for setting intentions about a specific question, inquiry, or desired action. Intention setting is different than trying to control outcomes because with intention setting, you're allowing the appropriate result to come to you when you ask. Intention setting often employs what Buddhists would call "non-attachment" because when you set an intention, you remain unattached to any outcome or answer that occurs. This means that sometimes the exact desired result may not occur for you, but that engaging with the deeper parts of the self (higher self or subconscious) brings the correct result for any given question. The reason for this is that the conscious mind may not already know the exact result, even if the higher self or subconscious mind does. In a later chapter we'll discuss the conscious and subconscious mind.

Incubation can be used as a question and answer dialogue process between you and the deeper parts of the psyche, which have access to the collective unconscious and already know the answer to the questions you are seeking.

The Dream Incubation process is a series of steps that you can do right before you retire to sleep. The detailed process will be outlined in Chapter 10. It can be used as often as you like, and even every night if you wish. The more you practice the incubation technique, the more the results will build momentum and you will find that your answers will arrive rapidly in response to your questions.

Dream Incubation also includes the process of recording dream content in a journal. Keeping a journal allows you to track dreams and patterns, work with dream symbols, and more. In a later chapter, the specific uses of your dream journal, which plays an integral part in the incubation process, will be discussed. Keeping a journal to record the details of your dreams is the final step in the Dream Incubation process.

The power of Dream Incubation cannot be underestimated. It's astonishing what can be achieved through this process and the wisdom that we can access through dreams. For example, a profound dream that I had after my son's birth detailed what was needed for birthing recovery. I had an emergency c-section and the recovery was difficult. I decided to use Dream Incubation to inquire what I needed to help the recovery process. In just one night, I dreamed of a vague dream with few details, but one specific word: "panchakarma." I knew that panchakarma was an ancient Ayurvedic technique of detoxification, but I had never done it before. After I heard the word in the dream, I decided to try it. It helped my recovery immensely.

My clients also report profound results using the Dream Incubation Technique, especially when used in an iterative way. I have had them share that the Incubation process has resulted in greater insights into relationships, creative projects, major life decisions such as whether to move house or start a new job, health issues, and more.

## *Journal Activities*

1. How do you believe your sleeping dreams might help you achieve your waking dreams?
2. In what areas do you feel you have "attachment" in your life?
3. In what areas do you feel you have "non-attachment" in your life?
4. If you could have a conversation with your higher self, what questions would you ask?

## *Chapter 2:*

# What Are Dreams?

What are dreams? There are many theories on the nature of dreams, many based in psychological theory and clinical studies, and others based on cultural practices, spiritual practices and ideologies, and even quantum mechanics.

Many people are fascinated with the nature of dreams because they are so closely linked with the nature of what we call consciousness, a topic that is constantly being studied for more finite answers. There are different theories about consciousness and how one's own awareness plays a role in consciousness, and dreams are just one part of this vast world. A look at the nature of dreams necessarily involves looking at theories of consciousness, quantum theory, phenomenology, existential theories, and theories on the nature of reality itself.

One idea is that dreams are simply mental projections, like mental pictures or movies that play in the mind like virtual images (Talbot, 1991). Another theory provides that dreams offer insight into a type of holographic model and can be a window into a parallel time, somewhat like a parallel life occurring alongside one's current life (Wolf, 1987).

Another theory suggests that dreams offer insight into past lives previously lived, and which can provide insight into the current life being lived (Lucas, 2005). Yet another theory states that dreams are scenes from a parallel dimension not necessarily one's other life, but rather, simply another reality or dimension (Hallman, 2007).

Dream content and attempts at understanding the meaning of dreams can take a differing approach than looking at the nature of dreams, although they are interrelated. A Jungian approach would look largely at content, symbols, archetypes, and synchronicities. Jung noted that dreams could come from the individual unconscious mind (also referred to as the subconscious) or what he called the collective unconscious, a universal repository of consciousness that all people can access.

Jung, who had theorized extensively about dreams, noted in his work that context of the dream was highly important. He provides that "The psychological context of dream contents consists in the web of associations in which the dream is naturally embedded." (Jung, 1974).

Sigmund Freud and Erich Fromm both postulate that the content of dreams is a product and projection of the subconscious mind and that dreams, therefore, are "expressions of the irrational, primitive strivings within us..." (Fromm, 1957). In this way, dreams describe in pictures and symbols what the conscious mind cannot yet fully understand or process. Dreams according to this hypothesis, then, become a way to help process emotions or events that are difficult for the conscious mind and emotions to process.

Although these theories differ, what is consistent across them is that when we dream, we are engaging the mind and body in time and space. Dreams are wholly biological, physiological, mental, and emotional, and they engage an expression or form of consciousness, which takes place in a referential framework of time and space. It makes for an intriguing and fascinating look at dreams, and also the larger context of our existence as human beings.

## Two Types of Dreams

I categorize dreams into two basic, overarching categories: daily processing and quantum. I find that using these two categories is most helpful to interpret the possible meanings of dreams and better understand dreams.

Daily processing dreams are one way for the mind to process the occurrences of the day's events. They can be rote or mundane, or equally exciting depending on a person's activity. They can include anything you have encountered on a given day.

These can also include the processing of emotions about a given event or experience. Depending on the magnitude of the emotions, the dreamscape can be affected to symbolically process happiness, anger, disappointment, excitement, and other emotions.

Daily processing dreams can also work to process intellectual content. The mind absorbs everything it is exposed to, even if the conscious awareness doesn't remember it all. This is one reason why advertisements work so well, for example. Because the mind will process and store all the data it encounters, it needs extra processing time during sleep to categorize and store what needs to be remembered and discard what it doesn't need.

During sleep, some studies have shown that the mind converts short-term memory to long-term memory (Schoch, et al. 2019). Still others refute this or state that the clinical research is inconclusive (Vertes, 2004). What remains is that sleep is a precious time for restoration of mind, body, and emotions.

Dreams that are not daily processing can be considered, quantum, metaphysical, or Psi, P-S-I. Some of these dreams can also be considered spiritual in nature.

Some quantum dreams can put us in touch with those who have passed on. Often dreams about those who have passed on are actual connections with their spirit. Anectdotal reports repeatedly appear to have in common similar elements in that these dreams include a white cloudlike substance surrounding the person, or a white cloud beneath their feet or covering the ground.

I consider lucid dreams as part of the quantum or Psi category of dreams because these types of dreams are part of a psychic phenomena that occurs within the larger realm of consciousness. Lucid dreams are those dreams during which the dreamer is consciously aware they are dreaming. Many report that they can control their lucid dreams with their thoughts, and therefore are interacting with their own dreams in real time.

Other quantum dreams include those that give the dreamer a snapshot of a parallel life, or a parallel dimension. I consider these as "Psi" dreams, too, because they often leave the dreamer with a feeling that they have been somewhere else—and perhaps they have. Dreamers who report the experience of interacting with parallel lives or parallel dimensions report feeling tired in the morning when they wake as if they hadn't slept at all.

What do you think? Are dreams simply daily processing? Quantum? Lucid? Perhaps they are a combination of all of these depending on the dream? The most interesting thing about decoding your dreams is that you get to decide!

## *Journal Activities*

1. Are your dreams mostly daily processing or quantum?
2. Have you ever had a lucid dream? If so, what happened in the dream?
3. Journal about your most memorable dream. What made it so memorable?

*Chapter 3:*

# A Brief History of Dream Practices

The history of dream practices is expansive, across thousands of years, and many cultures, including the Egyptians, the Greeks, Native American tribes, Africans, and others. These ancient people used rituals or temples for their dream practices. "The expectation was that a god or benevolent spirit would cause the dreamers, or incubants, to have dreams that would solve or lead to the resolution of physical or mental illness."

(Delaney, 1996). To commune with the Gods in the dreamtime, temples provided an appropriate place. These ancient peoples believed that during dreamtime the soul left the body and that dreams took place in another, possibly supernatural world. (Hughes, 2000).

The oldest written documents about dreams have origins in Egypt, then Mesopotamia, one such papyrus found near Deir el-Medina and now a part of the British Museum's collection (Beatty, 1930). The Egyptian culture often used dreams as divining tools that held much power and insight into daily life. They used dreams to inquire about certain outcomes, much like the Dream Incubation practice. They used dreams as a healing tool, and a way to connect to the higher self and to the Gods.

Many Egyptians had shamanic powers that they used alongside dreams as a way to heal others, or work metaphysically and psychically. They also used altars, precious gemstones, and the phases of the moon to guide their dreaming practice.

Ancient Greek and Roman cultures also believed that dreams had special and powerful meanings for both the dreamer and for others. Like the Egyptians, both these cultures had specific dream temples used for working with dreams. The Temple of Asklepios was one such center in Greece that was used for the purpose of dreaming.

These cultures knew that dream symbols and content held much power—more power than the awake, conscious mind.

In their practice, they required that dreamers who entered dream temples abstain from alcohol, drugs, and other altering substances for three days before entering. Clinical research has since documented that these substances can have an altering affect on dreams (Angarita et. al., 2016).

The Mayan peoples also had dream temples by which they worked with dreams. One such temple, located just outside Chichen Itza in Mexico, was a dream pyramid devoted to the practice of dreams. The Mayan people believed that all people dreamed each night even if they didn't remember their dreams (Hughes, 2000).

Medieval alchemists also used dreams to indicate areas of personal evolution. Alchemists were mystic people who were believed to transform raw metals into gold. Dreams were important to these practitioners because they were considered divining tools, and a means to personal evolution.

The Iroquois tribe, who inhabited the Great Lakes and northeastern area of United States and along the border of Canada, also gave great meaning to dreams. They believed that dreams were so powerful they used their dreams to help make decisions for their entire tribe. "The first business of the day in an Iroquois village was dream sharing, because it was assumed that dreams were messages from the spirits and the deeper self, and that they might contain guidance for the community as well as the individual." (Moss, 2005). Shaman would use a process like Dream

Incubation in order to engage with their dream content, the spirit realm, and elders who had passed on. They believed that dreams held the answers to questions they sought. Dreams for the Iroquois, because they are so closely connected to the spirit world, were one of the most powerful tools for divination.

In the early 20th century Carl Gustav Jung traveled to Africa to study native tribes and their approaches to psychology, spirituality, and dreams. He found that these tribes liked to act out their dreams like stage plays. He wrote about these studies in his own journals, which later informed his theories on psychology.

Modern cultures still revere dreams as an important part of life, including in India and the Middle East (Mascaro, 2017).

Modern dream practices, and in particular Dream Incubation, live on today, although these practices don't always look the same or provide the same exact steps ancient peoples took. We have evolved these practices to support evolving modern life. Modern dream practices may make use of an altar, a dream vision board, or quantum and Psi dreaming techniques.

Dr. Gayle Delaney in her book, *Living Your Dreams: The Classic Bestseller on Becoming Your Own Dream Expert*, has formulated a more modernized approach to Dream Incubation based on her clinical studies. Likewise, Robert Moss has outlined a Dream Incubation process in his work *Conscious Dreaming*.

Chapter 10 will outline the process that I have adapted, and from which I have iterated on the earlier techniques mentioned, based on the positive results my clients have achieved over the last decade.

## *Research Activities*

1. Which culture do you find interesting? Do some research on the internet to find out if that culture had any dreaming practices that are notable.
2. Who were the medieval alchemists? Do some internet research to find out why they practiced the way they did. How is that similar or different to ritualistic practices today?
3. Who was Carl Gustav Jung? Do some research on the internet to learn more about his theories and how they influenced modern dreaming practices.

*Chapter 4:*

# Brain Activity During Sleep

Brain waves are the electrical impulses generated by the body and from the brain. They are most often measured by electroencephalogram, also called EEG. Brain waves are denoted in Hertz (Hz), a measure of frequency. Different frequencies occur at different times and under differing conditions. There are four different primary frequency ranges, each which indicate a state of awareness in a person.

Beta waves, which range from approximately 12-35 Hz indicate the brain activity of someone who is awake and aware, going about their day. The Beta range indicates someone who is awake and performing normal activity.

The Alpha range, or approximately 8-12 Hz indicates someone who is awake but subdued. Perhaps this is a person who is completing slow activity, or doing something like sitting and reading a book. Alpha waves indicate relaxation, and can indicate a meditative state.

The Theta waves, which are approximately 4-7 Hz, indicate someone who is in a creative state, or perhaps meditating. One can achieve Theta frequencies while awake during a deep meditation, but these frequencies also occur in the N2 stage of sleep.

Delta frequencies are the slowest at 0.5-4 Hz, and indicate someone who is sleeping and in the stage of sleep called deep sleep or N3. In some instances, a person very adept at meditation may be able to sustain Delta frequencies while awake. Tibetan monks, for example, who are highly skilled at meditation, can achieve a Delta state while being wide awake. However, the deep state of meditation can also indicate another frequency range, the gamma range. One particular study of practicing Buddhists who had been given the same training and methodology that the Tibetans have been practicing for several thousands of years were able to achieve brain wave frequencies in the gamma range during meditation (Lutz, et. al., 2004). Gamma waves can also be noted during periods of intense concentration during the waking state (Patel, 2021). This frequency range is 35 Hz and above, a higher frequency than Beta waves.

Another more recent study has indicated the presence of gamma waves in animals during sleep, but the study was not able to detect this frequency in humans in during sleep (Valderrama et. al., 2012).

What is known this far, is that the brain cycles through each of the four phases of frequencies during sleep, beginning with Beta while awake, then Alpha, Theta, and then moving into Delta.

Sleep itself is categorized into four stages of rapid eye movement and non-rapid eye movement. These are also called, N1, N2, N3, and R or REM. The body and brain will cycle through these stages each night, moving through each cycle approximately every 90 minutes. In N1, the lightest stage of non-REM sleep, Alpha waves are present alongside changing frequency activity in the brain.

Next comes N2, the second phase of non-REM sleep, a deeper sleep than N1, with some Delta and some Theta

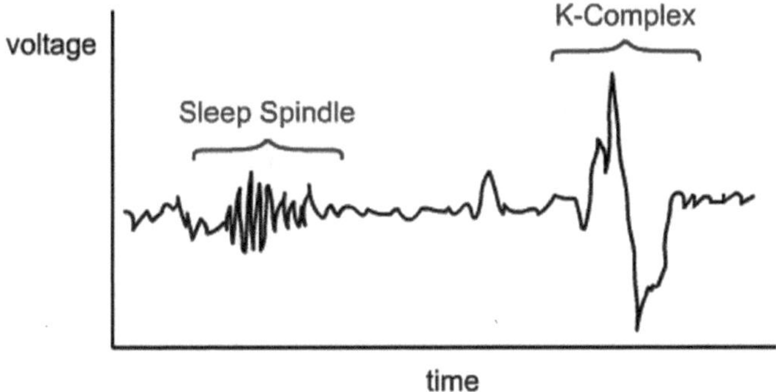


waves present. This is also the stage in which sleep spindles and K-complexes occur. Sleep spindles and K-complexes are alternating Theta waves followed by a quick increase in brain wave frequency called a K-complex (Patel, 2021). In clinical studies, sleep spindles have been documented to correlate with sleep-dependent memory consolidation (Nielsen, et. al., 2016).

N3, the deepest stage of sleep, comes next with brain wave frequencies square in the Delta range. During this phase breathing and heart rate have slowed. After N3, the brain and body move into REM, or rapid eye movement stage, where most dreaming occurs. The first REM phase typically will occur approximately 90 minutes after initially falling asleep. During this phase, the brain is highly active but the muscles of the body are temporary paralyzed, or atonic.

While dreams may occur during all stages of sleep, the most vivid dreams occur during the REM phases.

The amazing thing about dreams, and perhaps the most mysterious thing about dreams, is that during the REM phases of sleep, the brain functions at the same frequencies as it does when awake: approximately 12-35 Hz. A clinical study by J. Allan Hobson, David Kahn and colleagues (1998) indicates that REM stage of sleep can achieve brain wave frequencies as high or higher than the waking state. "The REM activated structures include the brainstem as well as limbic subcortex and cortex and their level of activation during REM can exceed that of waking. These new findings map onto the psychological data indicating that dream mentation is more bizarre, hallucinatory, amnesic and disoriented than waking consciousness." (Hobson et. al., 1998).

If the brain is as active during REM as it is when it's awake, it gives rise to many questions about dreams, the function and interpretation of dreams, and the phenomenological nature of dreams. This study lends to the conclusion that because of this increased frequency in brain wave activity during dreaming states, a person can perceive movement, emotional awareness, and the visual vividness of of waking life while still being immersed in the dream state. It changed our understanding of dreams and affirmed one explanation as to why dreams may be perceived so vividly by the dreamer.

It makes for a fascinating thing to ponder as it relates to what we know about consciousness and waking and sleeping states. Perhaps these states are not so different after all. And it may also support ideas about the quantum nature of dreams.

There are also two transitional phases that act like book-ends to the sleeping and dreaming phases: the hypnogogic state and the hypnopompic state. These are semi-conscious states in which some awareness can occur. These states are also the stages in which dreamers can acknowledge the feeling of sleep paralysis, and that feeling may also appear somehow as dream content.

The hypnogogic state is the phase going into sleep and the hypnopompic state is the phase coming out of sleep. "The term hypnagogic . . . from *hypnos* (sleep) and *agogeus* (leader) was introduced by Alfred Maury (1817–1892) in 1848." Shortly thereafter, the word hypnopompic was coined, "from *pompe* (act of sending) . . . by Frederic W.H. Myers (1843–1901) to describe these phenomena occurring during the transition between sleep and awakening." (Kompanje, 2008).

Regardless of whether you remember your dreams, you dream each night. Early clinical studies of brain waves correlated with sleep and dreaming phases led researchers to believe that dreams only occurred in the REM phase of sleep, but more recent studies show that dreams do occur in the NREM stages as well (Siclari, 2018). One amazing benefit of Dream Incubation is that it can help you remember your dreams each night, when practiced regularly.

### *Self Inventory Activities*

1. This week, try journaling your dreams if you wake up in the middle of the night. What differences do you see between the dreams you record in the middle of the night and the dreams that you journal in the morning?
2. Try Meditating this week. How is this experience similar or different from dreaming? Note your observations in your journal.

*Chapter 5:*

# The Conscious Mind

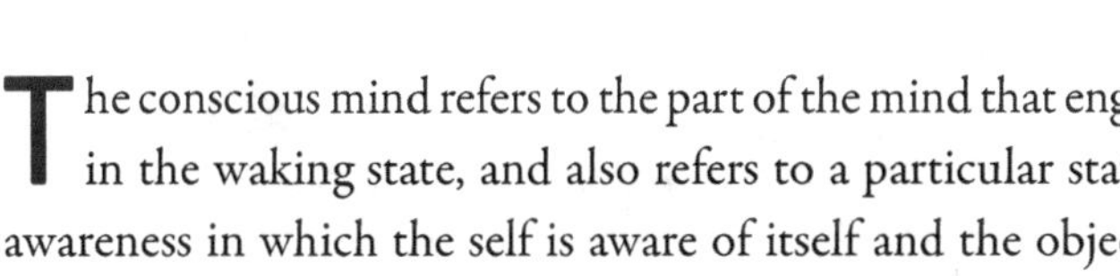

The conscious mind refers to the part of the mind that engages in the waking state, and also refers to a particular state of awareness in which the self is aware of itself and the objective external world. It is everything you experience in thoughts, feelings, and perception. The conscious mind is still being studied by psychologists, philosophers, and metaphysical practitioners as the body of scientific work describing "consciousness" grows. Much of this interesting topic is still a mystery, although recent studies have expanded our understanding of consciousness.

Philosophers throughout human history have attempted to explain the nature of consciousness and by way of consciousness also explain the nature of reality itself.

Martin Heidegger's work *Being and Time* discusses what we know as existential phenomenology, or the study of phenomena. Heidegger believed that beingness and time are inseparable. Moreover that being is time, and time is infinite. This, then, is how we come to understand what it means to be a human being.

Arthur Schopenhauer's body of work explored existential questions and reality to which he formulated his theories as "will" and "representation." That is, how the world appears, and what exists below that appearance.

*Martin Heidegger*

*Arthur Schopenhauer*

Recent breakthroughs in the field of consciousness include the work of Dean Radin and Masaru Emoto and colleagues, who studied the quantum effects of mental projections on water (Radin, et. al., 2008). In their particular study, approximately 2,000 people focused their power of intention on water crystals contained in an electromagnetically-sealed room. It was noted that these intentions had an aesthetic impact on the water samples and the way they appeared. This was groundbreaking in the field of quantum physics as it proved in a new way that the observer effects what is observed.

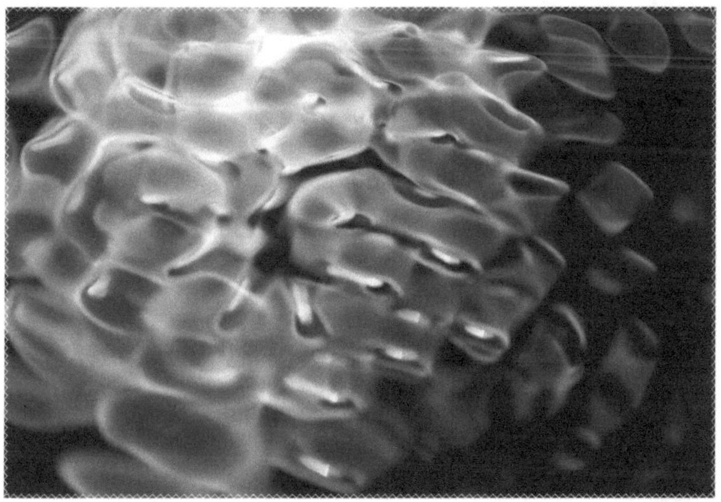

In his own individual studies, Emoto played different types of music to water and observed how their crystalline structure was affected. Those that were played heavy metal music showed disconnected, chaotic ripples.

Those that were played classical music showed harmonious patterns and ripples. His studies also showed that when people said positive words like joy, happiness, and love, the water responded positively. And when people said negative words like anger or hatred, the water also responded accordingly. This study shows the interrelatedness of things as well as the importance of the observer in cause and effect relationships.

Like Krippner's work in Dream Telepathy, which showed that dreamers could send telepathic messages to other dreamers in the sleeping state, this study shows a similar type of cause and effect relationship can occur in the waking state as well. Here we see again in another context, that characteristics of waking and dreaming states can be very similar and that setting intentions can have a powerful quantum effect.

Recent studies by Bruce Lipton have shown that the way we think can actually affect our health outcomes and even our DNA. Lipton's book, *The Biology of Belief* outlines this theory.

Gregg Braden, author of *The Divine Matrix* and *The Spontaneous Healing of Belief* both explore the quantum world and the effect that thinking has on our reality.

Dean Radin's work *Entangled Minds* explores the nature of psychic pheonomena and its relation to consciousness and reality. Radin asserts in his work that "reality is woven from strange holistic threads that aren't located precisely in space or time." He says "tug on a loose end from this fabric of reality and the whole cloth twitches instantly, throughout all time and space." What he means, then, is that everything is connected.

Michael Talbot in his book, *The Holographic Universe,* provides fascinating scientific evidence of quantum phenomena, including a special segment devoted to dreams and their Psi significance. In this work, he theorizes that the reality as we know it is nothing more than a type of projection from the mind, something like a holograph. And that this explanation finally rationalizes the Psi phenomena and quantum occurrences that were previously inexplicable.

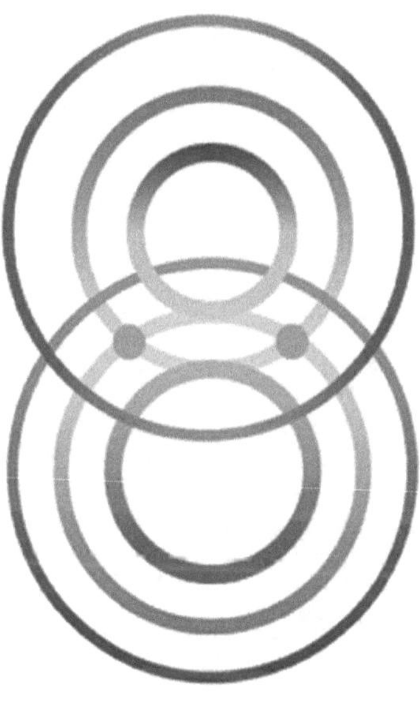

More recent studies are still searching for a unifying theory of consciousness that explains how the sensory and biological responses work together, such as the Global Neuronal Workspace theory (Koch, 2018). Still others have joined the conversation to make clear that all living beings possess consciousness, not just humans. Peter Wohlleben, author of *The Hidden Life of Trees* elucidates the complexity of this topic in his book.

What do you think? Is the universe, and therefore dreams, part of a holographic model? Are we able to change the structure of our DNA using mere thought? Can we better come to understand the world through our evolving understanding of consciousness? And, what does the conscious mind have to do with dreams?

These theories and studies about consciousness lend to the idea that we each can, with intention, impact not just thoughts but behavior—and even matter itself. That if we are to observe and intend for a particular cause and effect to occur, that perhaps it will in fact occur because of the interconnectedness of things. The Dream Incubation Technique engages the conscious mind as an intention is set during the process. If consciousness itself can respond to this intention, it's possible that we will see the cause and effect of the intention manifest in some observable way.

## *Research Activities*

1. Choose one book mentioned in this chapter and do more research on the topics discussed. How do these theories involve dreams? Do those theories change your view of dreams and the nature of dreams?
2. Navigate to YouTube and conduct a search for the terms "cymatics" or "Masaru Emoto." Take a look at the videos available about this. Record any interesting findings in your journal.

## *Chapter 6:*

# The Sub-Conscious Mind

The prefix "sub" means under. So, when we refer to the sub-conscious mind, we mean that which exists underneath the conscious mind. This is a vast world.

When something is subconscious, it means that we're not aware of it in the conscious mind. Freud in his theories referred to three levels of consciousness: unconscious, preconscious and conscious. Carl Gustav Jung referred to the subconscious mind as the unconscious mind, and modern psychology has adopted this term; however, many use the term subconscious as well.

"More than 90 percent of your mental life is subconscious." (Murphy, 2008). That means that the subconscious mind includes all of the "programs" that run behind the scenes of the conscious mind. To use a simplified analogy, think of the mind just like a computer processing data. The conscious mind could be the operating system, and the subconscious mind could be considered the raw data. If your computer runs on an operating system, then the conscious mind includes all the icons and programs on the desktop as part of that operating system. The subconscious mind, then, would be the computer coding language operating behind the scenes that makes the computer desktop operate for the computer user.

Carl Gustav Jung also referred to the subconscious mind, or the unconscious mind, as the individual unconscious. He identified that individuals have their own unconscious mind, but also that we are all connected through the collective unconscious, a vast pool of information that holds all of unconsciousness in it.

More recently, Dr. Joseph Murphy in his work, *The Power of Your Subconscious Mind*, more distinctly articulated the mechanisms of the subconscious mind and the ways in which it can influence the conscious mind. Whereas the conscious mind is the reasoning mind, the subconscious mind "accepts what is impressed upon it, or what your mind consciously believes." Further, it's important to note that the ". . . subconscious mind does not engage in proving whether your thoughts are good or bad, true or false." (Murphy, 2008).

The subconscious mind, then, is where all types of beliefs are stored indiscernibly. Some of these beliefs may be true, positive beliefs, and others may be negative or faulty. A faulty belief is a belief or thought form that is operating in the mind, typically from the subconscious mind, that isn't actually true. Faulty beliefs are also called limiting beliefs (Sisgold, 2013). Faulty beliefs are different from irrational beliefs in that they are typically very rational, but simply not accurate.

Faulty beliefs are based on an inaccurate conclusions that were derived from an observation or experience about which only partial information was accessible at the time of the experience. For example, a child may observe someone who is not paying attention to them and reading a book instead, and conclude that they themselves are ugly. When the accurate account is that the person is simply engaged in their own activity reading a book. An example such as this is how faulty beliefs are created. Another example may be conclusions that we come to about ourselves based on things like advertisements, such as, your life will be better if you purchase a particular type of car. A faulty belief that could be created based on this scenario may be something such as "My life will be bad if I don't have the right kind of car."

It's important to be able to examine our conscious thoughts and work with them wherever possible. Likewise it's important to work to discover the subconscious beliefs that we may hold. For the purposes of Dream Incubation, I use the terms subconscious and unconscious interchangeably because what is most important to the process is simply to delineate between that which we are aware, and that which we are unaware. We can begin to use the Dream Incubation Technique to work with the subconscious mind and its faulty beliefs—all the ideas, feelings and content of which we are unaware. When we make what is in the subconscious mind conscious, it no longer has the power to operate behind the scenes affecting behavior and choices. This could be one goal for using the Dream Incubation Technique.

## *Research Activities*

1. Conduct an internet search on "the subconscious mind." What important principles are necessary in order to understand how the subconscious mind works? Note these in your journal.
2. Conduct an internet search on "faulty beliefs." How do you think these inform your daily activities? How do you find that Dream Incubation can help reveal these beliefs? Note your answers in your journal.

*Chapter 7:*

# Modern Dream Theories

Modern Dream theories include those based on research from clinical psychologists and psychiatrists across a span of the last 150 years or so. There are many the world over who have contributed to what we know about the nature and function of dreams. This Chapter highlights a select list.

Sigmund Freud was an Austrian psychologist who lived during the late 19th and early 20th centuries. He was born in 1856 and lived until 1939. His psychological theories became widespread around the world as some of the first of their kind.

Freud is considered the founder of psychoanalysis, which we now know as psychotherapy—or a dialogue between psychologist and patient. His theories outlined a model of the psyche, the Id, the Ego, and the Super Ego, and described the unconscious, of which dreams are a part.

Freud published *An Interpretation of Dreams* in 1899. At the time, it was a groundbreaking book in the field of psychology.

*Sigmund Freud*

*Carl Gustav Jung*

*Fritz Perls*

Freud outlined his beliefs and observations of dreams in his patients and proposed a comprehensive theory about dreams.

Freud believed that dreams were representations of "wish fulfillment" and that dreams were a way of transporting the dreamer to a reality that played like a movie in the mind to show the wishes of the dreamer. So, for example, if a person wished to travel the world, but maybe didn't have the means to do so, they would find that their dreams were filled with adventures of exotic travel.

Carl Gustav Jung was a Swiss psychologist and an apprentice of Sigmund Freud. He studied under Freud until he found that his notions of dreams and psychology were different and more expansive than Freud's. Jung later continued on with his own theories, which were largely informed by his Christian faith.

Jung's work, *Memories, Dreams, Reflections*, was first published in German in 1962. It was a semi-autobiographical work that indicated Jung's theories and experiences with his own dream material. Jung believed that dreams were not just about wish fulfillment, but rather that dreams carried a deeper symbolic meaning unique to the individual dreamer that could be decoded for greater meaning.

Jung also believed that dreams were just one way to access what he called the collective unconscious, a strata of psychic energy to which all people are connected and can access. Another key component to Jung's theories is the phenomenon of synchronicity. His theory of synchronicity came as an outgrowth of his investigation of the collective unconscious. Jung states "What I found were 'coincidences' which were connected so meaningfully that their 'chance' concurrence would represent a degree of improbability that would have to be expressed by an astronomical figure."(Jung, 1973). Meaning that key coincidences were so closely linked by an unknown cause that statistically would be unlikely to occur at all—and yet they still did. This mysterious but recurrent phenomenon later became what he called synchronicity, a term still used today. Jung noted in his work that synchronicities could occur in the waking state and between the waking and dreaming states.

Fritz Perls, founder of Gestalt Therapy, lived from 1893-1970. Alongside the studies of Carl Gustav Jung, his work has lived on into the modern era. Perls published his book called *Gestalt Therapy* in 1951, and this work described a method that looks holistically at the psyche based on the idea that people experience things as a whole, not in parts (Vedfelt, 1999). He was associated with the Esalen institute, which still thrives in California today.

Ole Vedfelt in his compendium *The Dimensions of Dreams* describes Perls' theory as the "royal road" to psychological integration. The theory was based on the idea that the parts of the dream were different aspects of the dreamer's personality, and when understood, could help the dreamer integrate all these aspects.

Vedfelt further theorizes that dreams as existential communication are clues to how a dreamer is relating to his or her own life, and when understood, can provide a feasible path to personal evolution.

Another modern psychological theorist, Erich Fromm, who lived from 1900-1980, contributed to psychological and dreaming theories by describing what he called one universal symbol language. Fromm's theories detailed three types of symbols that could occur in dreams: conventional, accidental, and universal. Conventional and universal symbols each have a single specific but universal meaning for all people. The accidental symbols are those that reflect something personal and unique to the dreamer (Fromm, 1957).

There are many others, too, who have impacted dream studies in the last several decades. Stanley Krippner is a modern American psychologist who has done extensive studies in dreamwork. He was born in 1932, and has been a significant contributing member of the International Association for the Study of Dreams. His work is known the world over, and he continues to dig deeper into the dreamworld with his current studies and theories.

In 1985, Krippner embarked upon a study to investigate psychic phenomena during dream time. Working with Montague Ullman, MD, and Alan Vaughn, their studies indicated that individual dreamers could, in fact, relay or transmit information to one another during dream time. Their book, *Dream Telepathy: Experiments in Nocturnal Extrasensory Perception* outlines these studies.

Renowned psychologist Gayle Delaney has contributed greatly to studies on dreams, including the first clinical studies ever done on Dream Incubation. She was one of the co-founders of the Association for the Study of Dreams in 1983, and the nonprofit organization has lived on since. The organization is now called the International Association for the Study of Dreams and champions multidisciplinary approaches to dreams and the investigation of dreams and dreaming.

The International Association for the Study of Dreams, an organization of which I, too, am a member, offers membership to those who are interested in dreams, and those who actively study the nature of dreams. The IASD is a worldwide organization with regional groups around the globe. They offer conferences and scientific research on the latest dream investigations being conducted.

More recent studies exploring the nature of the reality of dreams include everything from the average person's dream journals to the most high-tech professional studies being completed the world over.

A presentation that I delivered to the International Association for the Study of Dreams postulated that there is correlation between the colors we dream and the relationship between the chakras (invisible energetic centers of the body) and these colors. When interpreting possible meanings for a given dream, the color or colors indicated provide additional meaning for the dream's context.

Chris McCleary did a recent study on how dreamers could collectively work to dream and predict with accuracy future newspaper headlines. Hosted by the National Dream Center, his team showed that there was an 84% incidence of accuracy for these predictions, and often dreamers shared the same or similar information regarding one particular headline.

Ryan Hurd did a study on ley lines and how these interesting places around the world affect dreaming. He notioned that dreams had an effect on archaeology via older cultures and their cave art. He found that ley lines, or energetic lines across the Earth had an impact on cave paintings and therefore influenced the way of life of ancient peoples.

Robert Moss, dream expert in cultural and historical traditions of dreams the world over, has published many books not just on the history of dreams, but on dreamwork practices for the modern era. *Active Dreaming*, one of his titles, offers ways to integrate dreamwork into the waking life in order to expand the possibilities of choice in waking life. His work, *Dreamways of the Iroquois*, extensively details Native shamanic traditions and their importance to our understanding of the use and meaning of dreams within a larger historical context of dreaming.

Ted Andrews, author of *Dream Alchemy*, offers a more esoteric look at the use and importance of dreams. His work builds on Jung's archetypal work and adds to it a blend of shamanic and new age spiritual practices such as using herbs, crystals, flower essences, and more. He regards the dream state as a separate reality beyond waking consciousness through which we interact with the subtle energetic bodies (Andrews, 1991).

Denise Linn, the founder of the Gateway Dreaming™ coaching certification program and author of *The Hidden Power of Dreams*, has a similar approach to Ted Andrews' *Dream Alchemy*. Linn's work also makes use of her Native Cherokee traditions, and the Chinese clock, which correlates to the major organs of the body through different times of day. In addition, her work also uses the practice of guided meditations and the process of creative visualizations to guide the Dream Incubation process (Linn, 2009).

What's next for dreaming studies? There is a lot yet to be discovered. The information available is incredibly vast and only continues to grow, which is why dreams continue to be such an intriguing topic of study. What we can conclude based on the research of modern theorists, is that dreams are not just personal, but they can also be collective. They are an indication of a greater connection between all beings. And that people do have the power to influence their dreams, and harness that power for something good.

## *Research Activities*

1. Choose one of the theorists mentioned in this chapter and conduct an internet search on their theories. Note any interesting facts in your journal.
2. Visit the National Dream Center's website. Submit one of your dreams, if you like.
3. Visit http://kellybulkeley.org/ and the Sleep and Dream database. Choose a couple of key words from your own dreams and conduct a search. What does the database reveal? How are these similar or different from your dreams?

*Chapter 8:*

# Tools for a Dream Practice

It's easy to begin a dream practice and you need only a few simple tools to begin working with dreams.

First, a journal where you can record your dreams is essential. Many people like to find a particular type of journal, or something that is fancy or ornate. I suggest choosing something that is inspiring and aesthetically pleasing as this will inspire you to use the journal more frequently.

Second, you'll need an incubation container. This can be something that you make, or something that you purchase. Make sure that whether you make the container or purchase something, that it is small and that it has a lid. Some like to use the small paper-mache boxes found at craft stores so that they can be decorated in a personal way. The material doesn't matter; however, I have found that natural materials seem to be more relaxing and inspiring, and your own demeanor can influence your dreams.

Extra paper is essential as you'll be crafting your statements of intention on these and using them with your chosen incubation container. I like to use a colored paper that has a design on it. Plain paper or lined paper is fine, too. Just make sure that you like the kind of paper that you are using as you will be infusing this paper with your intentions and positive thoughts for incubation results.

You'll need a pen, of course, that you will use to record your dreams and thoughts in your journal. You'll also need a pen to use with your small scraps of paper, which will be placed in your incubation container.

Lastly, I suggest colored pencils or markers to use with your dream journal and with your small pieces of paper. Some find that more elaborate drawings are inspiring and help facilitate the Dream Incubation process.

Once you have all of these items, you'll be ready to begin the process. I recommend storing these in the bedroom, somewhere near the bed, such as on a night table, or dresser.

## Your Dream Incubation Container

Your Dream Incubation container should be something to which you are visually drawn. Some people like to craft their own, and others like to purchase something pre-made. My incubation container is a small wooden box with a lid and a small turquoise gemstone embedded in the lid. It's approximately 2" in diameter and is round in shape.

Your container can be any shape. I like round containers because I am naturally drawn to the circular shape. Choose a shape that resonates with you and that you feel will amplify your dream practice. Just be sure that your container has a lid. This is because you'll be using the container to energetically infuse your intentions and you want to symbolically contain the energy when the intentions are set. This can offer a more powerful outcome.

Your Dream Incubation container can be made of any material. I prefer natural materials rather than plastic, but this is completely up to you. I recommend that you choose something that you find pleasing to look at, as you'll be using it often and infusing it with your positive thoughts. Your container will be placed near the bedside each night that you use it.

I recommend a smaller sized container as it will be used to contain your intention and energy, and a smaller container will make it more powerful. I recommend no more than 5-6" wide, unless you intend to place other items in your incubation container. This is optional but not required for the technique to work. Some like to place crystals or other talismans in their incubation container to support their intention setting. Do what you feel is right for you and what is right for where you are in your dreamwork process. You can always make small changes to your process as time progresses and your level of insight changes.

## The Dream Journal

Your dream journal has an important part in the incubation process.

I recommend using a dream journal each night and each morning to capture any pertinent details that you want to remember.

Upon waking you'll want to record the details of your dreams to begin decoding their meaning.

Then, during waking hours, record relevant experiences that occur, especially those that seem impactful. This could be something that you find interesting, emotionally engaging, or out of the ordinary.

When you record the details of your dreams, try to be as precise as possible. Many dreams appear to occur like a movie unfolding in the mind. They have characters, setting, and a kind of "plot." Dreams need not be long to have all these elements, even short dream fragments will contain a context about a person or setting. When you begin recording the details of your dreams, write what happens chronologically, as if recounting a story to another person. Don't leave out any specific or relevant actions as these may reveal greater meaning later.

## Recording Elements for Interpretation

Include descriptions of the people who appear in your dreams in your dream journal. Are they tall? Short? Male? Female? How many people are present in the dream? What are they doing? Do any of them say anything to you? If so, what? People in dreams can be actual people that you know in your life, or they may be characters you've never seen before. Each is important to decoding your dream's meaning, and all should be described in your journal.

Take note of any colors that you see in your dreams. It's rare that a person dreams in black and white—most people dream in color (Schwitzgebel, 2002). Colors in dreams can indicate different meanings, depending on their context. Red, for example, may mean energy or vitality. Purple can mean wisdom or clarity of mind. Orange may indicate power struggles, or a lack of motivation. Each hue has great meaning in the context of the dream.

Animals in dreams can hold special meaning, too. Some who use shamanic practices identify animals as specific totems, gifting us with wisdom through dreams. Spiders, for example, can mean creativity and newness. Wolves can mean ferocity, wisdom, or interpersonal issues.

Numbers can have great symbology as well. The number 1 can symbolize oneness with the higher self, or it can mean selfishness. The number 5, for example, can indicate a strong feminine connection. The number 11 can also mean alignment with the higher self. Record all numbers that appear in your dreams, and also note if these same numbers appear during the waking life following the dream. Make note of these in your dream journal.

Setting and location can indicate emotional states, or can have a literal meaning. Location, such as the beach, for example, may indicate a need for more rest and relaxation, or can mean that a dreamer is facing difficult emotions. A forest setting may mean that a person is feeling safe or connected to nature. A warehouse setting may mean that the dreamer feels lost or alone, or has untapped creative potential waiting to be utilized.

## Recording Waking Life Elements

It's also important to record relevant experiences from the waking time alongside your entries about the dreamtime.

Dreams that fall into the daily processing category can include real experiences that have recently happened during waking time. Be sure to record any daily experiences that you feel are important, meaningful, or feel related to any dreams you have had.

Also record in your journal any major life events that occur as you begin your dream practice. I always date each entry in my dream journal so that I can see what is occurring in a chronological way. Where the dreams intersect with waking life is an important thing to notice.

Make note of any strange coincidences, too, as these are signals that the process is working! These are what Carl Gustav Jung called synchronicities, the events that appear to have no causal relationship, but are nevertheless somehow related in a meaningful way. We usually think of synchronicities as strange coincidences. For example, maybe a friend that you dream of suddenly calls you after you haven't heard from them in a few years. Or, maybe you dream of a song, and then wake up and hear that song on the radio the next morning. Synchronicites are often accompanied by a magical feeling or a feeling of inexplicable mystery. They put us in touch with the ineffable in life. They are significant, and they are signs that the process is working. When synchronicites occur, always write them in your journal.

Lastly, be sure to record anything that feels important to you. Each person will experience something slightly different with this process, and that is expected. What feels important to you is important to the process. Trust the process and trust yourself and you'll be decoding your dreams and manifesting symbol answers in no time at all.

## Additional Uses of Your Journal

Your dream journal may include additional musings as well. Some like to sketch illustrations of their dreams in their dream journal. You need not be an artist in order to do this, and often a visual queue can have a big impact on remembering details of dreams.

Your journal is a personal artifact that you will use to record your dream content and symbols. No one needs to see your journal unless you give them permission to view it or decide to share it directly. Your dream journal should also be a place of non-judgment. Draw what feels important to you and this will help you decode your dream meanings.

Fictitious settings will be different than any city or landscape you know. Sketch a map of the setting that appeared in the dream to get a bird's eye view of it. Maps need not be replicas of locations that already exist. The mind's eye is more creative than we can imagine.

Landscapes can be wondrous, large, small, or even magical places. Sketch the landscape that appears in your dream to reconnect with it. Plants, mountains, streams, and lakes can all become unique in the dreamscape.

You may like to write about feelings in the dream journal as well. The dreamscape can reveal unacknowledged feelings as well as help process feelings that are already present. Writing about them helps to process the feelings more quickly, and it helps to bring greater meaning and depth to your waking experience when feelings are explored.

## Beyond Dreams

Keep in mind that your dream journal can be used to write about additional, related topics, such as:

- Goal Setting
- Project Planning
- Ah-ha! Moments

Many of the waking life goals that you have can be impacted by the Dream Incubation Technique. Being as clear as possible about your goals and aspirations in your journal can help to guide the incubation process and the actionable steps you may choose to take as a result of your dream's answers in the waking life. You can also record in your journal key milestones toward your goals and the steps you achieve along the way as a way to track your ongoing self-awareness and personal evolutionary progress.

*Chapter 9:*

# The Dream Incubation Process

The Dream Incubation process is simple, effective, and easy to do. Some even wonder why, or how, if it is so simple, that it could actually work. With time and with practice, the incubation process can enhance your dream memories by more than 50% and work with your intentions to bring answers to your inquiries. You can frame your incubation as a question or statement, noting that questions tend to be more powerful. The example here will offer you the process in the question form. The process outlined here is an updated iteration of previous techniques based on more than a decade of work coaching clients to their highest potential.

*Step One:* First, you'll want to frame the question. It's important *not* to use questions that have simple yes/no answers. Rather, frame your questions so that they are open ended. Examples may include something like: What do I need to know about my health? How can I increase abundance? What skills do I need to increase to move into my next job? How can I increase my personal vibration? Once the question is asked, remain open to receiving whatever answers may come through the dream.

*Step Two:* Once you have formulated your question, write the question on a small piece of paper.

*Step Three:* Then, fold the paper so that your writing is not visible on the outside.

*Step Four:* Place your paper in your Dream Incubation container, and secure the lid. This "contains" the intention you wish to bring forward in order to answer your question.

*Step Five:* Sit at the edge of your bed, with your dream container in hand. I recommend using both hands, and simply let the container rest in a calm position.

Repeat the question that you wrote on your paper at least three times. You can say this to yourself in your mind, or aloud for greater amplification.

Once you have recited your question, place your Dream Incubation container at your bedside, on a bedside table, or similar. It's important never to place your container on the ground as this will slow the frequency of your intention, and therefore your result.

*Step Six:* Once you retire into bed, silently focus on your question as you wrote it on the paper in your Dream Incubation container. Do this for at least five minutes as you drift off to sleep.

Relax as you retire to sleep and allow the incubation process to unfold in a natural way.

## How to Use Dream Incubation

The Dream Incubation Technique works best if you practice this at least three times per week to begin. Many will like to practice this every day as this primes your subconscious mind, prepares the conscious mind, and bridges this connection faster the more you practice.

Practice with this will help enhance your dream memories, so it's important to be consistent in your practice.

It's important to use the incubation process in an incremental way. You will achieve the best and most rapid results this way. For instance, when you are framing a question for incubation, you may ask: *What is the appropriate next step to take to finding my dream job?* A question like that rather than: *What is my dream job?* will be more effective.

One of the most important things you can do is have compassion for yourself as you work through this process. Although simple, Dream Incubation is a very powerful technique to reveal the workings of your subconscious mind—which is where blocks to success, creativity, and abundance can be. The more compassion you can have for yourself throughout this process, the more rapidly will you see your results.

And lastly, be open to whatever results occur. Sometimes, the subconscious mind will reveal memories that are painful or unpleasant. Embrace these, because if they are surfacing, it is only in order that they be processed and released so that you can move forward in a more expansive way. Be welcoming to rapid positive results, too. Often we feel we have to work hard to achieve great results and that is not necessarily the case. Be open and trust that whatever is supposed to show up with this process is the exact right thing at the exact right time.

### *Dream Tending Inventory*

- *What colors are present in your dream?*
- *Where do these colors they appear?*
- *What people, if any, appear in the dream?*
- *What animals, if any, appear in the dream?*
- *What emotions are present in the dream? In what context did these emotions appear?*
- *What important events are occurring in your waking life right now?*
- *What parallels do you find between your dream and the waking life?*
- *What new insights does this dream provide?*

Use your journal to further decode your personal dream symbols using the suggestions mentioned in the chapter.

*Chapter 10:*

# Framing Incubation Language & Setting Intentions

What does it mean to set an intention?

Intention setting is one of the key components of the Dream Incubation practice. While the ancients used ritual to invoke incubation and a visit from the Gods, a modern approach can use intention, in a similar way that Emoto used intention in his studies with water crystals.

"In all inner work . . . it is intention, not ritual, that matters. If you have a questions you truly need answered, you can take it to your dream sources." (Moss, 1996). Intention is the emotional component of the practice, and that which we use to engage the linguistic component that works with the conscious and subconscious mind in a kind of dialogue.

When you set intentions, it is important to do so without the expectation of a particular result. This seems like a paradox doesn't it? How can you set intentions for a desired outcome and at the same time know that the outcome you are asking for may not occur? Then, what's the point? Well, as soon as you begin to engage in a dialogue with the mind, the *correct* answers will come to you. Intention setting does require a great deal of trust. A trust in the knowing that whatever is in your highest good will come to you by way of the answer to the questions you ask.

Think again about the Buddhist concept of non-attachment. This is exactly the kind of mindset required for the highest, most effective answer to come to you. Trust that the higher self and the subconscious mind already know the answers to the questions that you are seeking to understand. It's amazing what can occur if you let go and trust.

*Intention setting works with a statement or a question, although questions are more effective.*

Specifically framing the language used with your intention is the other key component of Dream Incubation.

Intention setting uses specific language to request of the conscious mind to the subconscious mind and the higher self for a particular dreaming experience, and a particular answer to a question.

In my work with my clients, I have seen answers occur in just 1-2 attempts at this process. I have also seen that some questions remain unanswered for a time and then appear at a later time. Trust that what occurs to you is the exact right thing at the exact right time. Remember, when you set intentions, part of that is being comfortable with letting go.

## Framing Your Questions

Framing your questions is an important part of the Dream Incubation Technique as you'll often be communicating with your subconscious mind. The subconscious mind primarily hears verbs, so it's important to choose the verbs you use carefully. The subconscious also cross references your incubation questions to old memories and beliefs. With this technique, you can begin to utilize your intentions setting and question framing to uncover the "faulty beliefs" that are stored in the subconscious mind. These beliefs can create blockages beyond your conscious mind's awareness that slow or hinder progress of personal growth. With the Dream Incubation Technique, you can begin to better understand these faulty beliefs and uncover ways to release them.

This is why it's so important to steer clear of questions that can be answered with a simple yes/no reply. Instead ask open-ended questions that are a bit more complex. Combined with the energy of intention setting, your dreams will reveal to you the answers in their own symbolic language that you can learn to decode.

## Examples of Effective Questions Include:

- What do I need to know about increasing my health and vitality?
- What next step should I take to advance my career?
- What does my higher self need to communicate about creativity?

You may also use statements instead of questions, although these are not as powerful as asking questions. Examples of effective statements can include:

- ▶ Tonight I will lucid dream.
- ▶ Tonight I will dream of reconnecting with my loved one.
- ▶ Tonight my higher self will guide me to the answers I need to most understand right now.

Remember the most powerful questions and statements allow the space for any answer to be acceptable. Be open to whatever the collective unconscious will convey, and whatever your higher self will convey in order to receive the answers you seek.

## Timing & Practice

Timing and practice are key to the Dream Incubation process. It's important to be mindful of timing for two reasons.

The higher self knows what's best at any given time. That means that the answers that arrive to you are the exact right answers at the exact right time. As with intention setting, moving into a space of trust and letting go is so very important. The same is true for timing. Trying hard, or making a huge effort by spending too much mental energy on a particular question throughout the day is *not* effective. This can actually create even more blocks and add stress to the process. Leave your incubation process to the higher self when you sleep, and don't think about it too much during the day. Ask the question that you are drawn to ask at a given time. Do not spend time deliberating on the perfect question. Ask, set the intention, then let go.

The subconscious mind may have stored faulty beliefs. Part of what occurs with the Dream Incubation process is that these faulty beliefs can begin to be released. Everyone has faulty beliefs, and these are a product of misinterpreted information that is stored in memory in such a way that we perceive in a particular way. It's kind of like the example of rose-colored glasses. Faulty beliefs are a filter to the daily experiences that occur. Trust that whatever is being revealed at a given time is the exact right thing for you at that exact time. Don't second guess any faulty beliefs, or try to pick them apart during the day. Allow the incubation process to work on its own, and let go during the daytime as much as you do during sleep.

Remember that each person is different and, therefore, results will differ for everyone. We all are a compendium of our unique experiences and our faulty beliefs. And that's what makes us beautiful and human. Try not to judge yourself during this process.

If at first you're not remembering your dreams as rapidly as you'd like, don't give it second thoughts—and certainly don't ruminate on it or feel bad. Each person has their own best timing and the higher self and subconscious mind know this. Applaud yourself instead for beginning a practice that will bring you greater self-awareness and understanding.

## *Practice with Prompts (Statements & Questions)*

It's important to frame your statements and questions for Dream Incubation in a succinct manner. Remember the mind accesses and hooks onto the verb part of language, so keep that in mind as you begin.

Fill in the blanks for the following:

1. Tonight I will dream of ______________________.
2. What would my subconscious mind like to tell me about ______________________?
3. What awareness does my subconscious mind hold about ______________________?
4. How do I feel about ______________________?
5. When ______________________ comes to mind, how do I feel?
6. What do I need to know about ______________________?
7. What would my dreams like to tell me about ______________________?
8. Tonight my subconscious mind will give me clues about ______________________.

When you feel comfortable with the above, try writing some of your own.

Practice each day with 1-3 questions or statements and you will quickly become good at writing your incubation prompts!

## *Chapter 11:*

# Advanced Dream Incubation Techniques

In earlier Chapters, the differing theories of dreams were briefly outlined. Carl Gustav Jung's theories were mentioned as was his concept of synchronicity. In my many years (more than a decade) of coaching people I have found truth in Jung's theories, particularly in that there is a larger unified field to which we are all connected. Jung called this the collective unconscious, some refer to it as a universal life force that courses through all living things, some call it God. To me it makes no difference the label that one uses, but that we acknowledge it exists. I also have found that the mechanism in the psyche that functions as the subconscious—or the individual unconscious—plays a strong role in each person's beliefs, thoughts, feelings, actions and behavior, and ultimately the destiny that's created day by day.

As well, Jung referred to a part of the unconscious as the "shadow" the part of ourselves which we do not and cannot know except or unless the symbols of the unconscious are decoded in some way. Jung often looked to dreams for these symbols and their meaning. I recall an early misunderstanding I had of the concept of the shadow, back in college when I first began studying Jung and his work. I misinterpreted shadow to simply mean the dark or destructive part or nature of the psyche. But that interpretation makes the shadow more akin to Freud's Thanatos drive. That was not the totality of the concept.

Later with more study, and some of my own personal evolution and insight, I realized that was not the case; the shadow was not necessarily the dark or "bad" parts of the psyche, the parts of the person that one could try to suppress because they were unfavorable or less than ideal. This inaccurate interpretation was about not acknowledging those parts, suppressing them out of shame—the exact opposite of transformative work that can serve to evolve awareness.

A better understanding of the shadow is simply that which is unknown. Not that it can never be known, perhaps only in part, but that there is a portion of awareness that is hidden amongst the shadows in the unconscious.

The most amazing thing I have found about the Dream Incubation Technique is that it provides a rapid access point to the subconscious content, and in particular to the content of the shadow part of the psyche. The dreams, then, can be used to decode the deeper truths of which we are not aware in order to become more aware. I do not believe that anyone can make effective or lasting change in waking life without a growing awareness of the self. This is an ever-evolving process.

The Dream Incubation Technique can help to uncover what is unconscious, what is in shadow, and support the process of awakening a greater awareness from within. Used in an ongoing and iterative way, Dream Incubation can work very rapidly, too.

The more one becomes aware, the more available a greater awareness becomes. It appears to unfold in a natural way, replete with "ah-ha moments," each one that leads to the next insight in an easy way. Then, once a greater awareness is achieved, lasting change can begin to be enacted in whatever form it may take—or whatever form a person chooses to enact in their waking life.

An advanced approach to Dream Incubation can involve an iterative process such that the questions asked or the statements of intention that are used, follow an evolving and iterative pattern. As subsequent insights are gained, the question or statement then can be changed to support the next new insight to be revealed through these symbols.

This iterative process is an advanced approach that you can do once you have gained a deep level of insight into your personal dream symbols, their meanings, and what those meanings reveal about your individual consciousness.

## Advanced Techniques in Practice

A woman who is unsure of her career path decides to try the incubation process. She has been working in jobs she doesn't love, and wants a change. She formulates the question: What is the next step in my career path? That night she has the following dream:

> *I am standing in a warehouse that is dark. I can see there are shelves and some of them are bare and some have boxes on them. The ceiling above is very tall and there are lights hanging from it. The lights are off. I walk toward the shelves and see that there are some boxes that are sealed with tape and others that are open. All of them are dirty. A small mouse scurries across the floor and runs under one of the shelves. I hear a voice behind me*

*and turn around to see my old high school art teacher standing there. He says to me "You've gotten older and your fingers are wrinkled." I turn from him and run toward the door of the warehouse. When I get there, I fling it open and a bright, bright light floods over me. Then I wake up.*

After reflecting on the dream, the woman reminisces that she used to love art and was very talented. She didn't pursue a career in art for many reasons, but always loved it. Her interpretation of the dream and internal self-exploration reveals this:

- The dirty boxes are symbolic of untapped potential
- The warehouse is symbolic of her greater potential
- The mouse is symbolic of her fear of her own potential
- The teacher is her inner voice, supporting her to a higher potential
- The teacher is also symbolic of her own fear of her potential
- She decides that she needs to tap into her creativity and return to art
- She's still unsure if the dream is asking her to make art her career or simply use the artistic process to help guide her way to her next career step

The answer to the question is unclear, but the dream reveals many clues.

The next night, the woman returns to incubation. This time, she changes her incubation question to build upon the dream that she had about the warehouse. She asks: What can my dream reveal about my fear of my own potential?

That night the woman dreams:

*I am a young child again, sitting on a picnic blanket on a grassy hill. The sun is shining brightly and I can see flowers around the hedge of a house that is off to the right. The house is white. I am playing with a toy that was my favorite toy as a child. It's rainbow-colored and has a flap that you open to reveal a hidden doll inside. I remember this toy well, and used to pretend I was the doll inside. Then, the neighboring children see me and come over to my picnic blanket. My mother is also there, sitting next to me. One of the children wants my toy and grabs it from my hand. He takes it and begins to run. I start to cry.*

After reflecting on this dream, the woman decodes the following:

- The toy is symbolic of her potential career
- The doll inside the toy is a symbol of she herself
- The neighboring child who takes the toy is symbolic of what the woman fears: that she cannot trust others and feels uncomfortable being vulnerable
- The house is symbolic of the woman's deeper desire to have a career that allows her to express herself more fully

After self-reflecting, the woman believes the answer to the Dream Incubation question to be that her fear of vulnerability with people and her lack of trust impacts her greatest career potential. She sees the dream as a message reminding her that she wants to expand her career, yet she has fear around how to expand so that she can feel safe. She believes that most people are like the boy child who took her toy, they want to exploit her talent for their own purposes and leave her with nothing.

As you can see from this example, the second dream, which was more specific built upon the first dream in an iterative way. Additionally, the second dream revealed to the dreamer an underlying belief that she had about her potential, about her trust in others to support her potential and talents, and why she was holding herself back. The information revealed in the dream then provides choices for the dreamer: Shall she continue with the incubation process and reveal more? Can she work on trusting people in her waking life? Will she choose to work to dispel her fears and move forward on a new, more expansive path?

It also brings further questions: Why doesn't she trust others and is she willing to open to trust? Will she choose to use creativity to support her fullest potential? What does she need to do mentally and emotionally to begin to trust others again? Are there other related factors that these two dreams have not yet revealed and should other potential factors be explored further?

This example indicates that the questioning process is as important as the interpretation of the symbols in the incubation process. During my tenure as a dream coach I have seen that many people's dream symbols contain both a mix of highly personal symbols and some universal symbols as well. The process of understanding your own personal dream symbols can be both analytical and intuitive, too. Sometimes the meaning of a dream is known upon waking, seemingly without explanation. It's important to trust those types of feelings, too. Each dream will be unique and highly contextual—part of the adventure that dreams present.

Many people use incubation with a specific purpose when they need it and then take a rest from the practice at times. It's fine to let your personal process move with a natural ebb and flow. There will naturally be periods of more intense inquiry and periods of less inquiry. During periods of more intense inquiry it is important to commit to the Dream Incubation process so that the iterations can build upon one another and reveal the information about which you're inquiring. Then, when those questions feel complete, you may wish to take a break from Incubation. With practice and time, many people find their own rhythm with the practice that works well for them.

## *Chapter 12:*

# Tips for Rapid Results

Here are some last thoughts as you begin your own Dream Incubation process. I hope you find these helpful to your practice.

The process is deceivingly simple.

- The process amplifies with practice and time.
- You are creating a bridge between the conscious mind and unconscious mind.
- Your higher self has access to the collective unconscious, and to the highest divine wisdom.

Lastly, believe in the power of intention. It has the potential to provide everything you've dreamed of.

- Never place your incubation container on the floor.
- Drink a half-glass of water before retiring.
- Refrain from caffeine, drug, or alcohol consumption.
- Believe in the power of intention.

# Bonus Material

To receive a bonus mp3 download called "Dream Incubation Meditation" that can be used with your Dream Incubation practice, visit: www.kellylydick.com and sign up for Kelly's *Fields of Dreams* newsletter.

You can hear an interview with Kelly on Speak Up Talk Radio, here: https://www.speakuptalkradio.com/kelly-lydick-speaksup/

# Acknowledgments

Many thanks to many people for their support and insight in the creation of this book. First Dr. Gayle Delaney for her kindness and openness to support this work. Dr. David Kahn, whose keen eye helped me to see where I needed to refine my language to provide the intended messages and communication I was reaching to provide. Dr. Stanley Krippner for his insight and feedback into the clinical components mentioned. Robert Moss, for his sprightly candor and not so gentle nudging to push my work further so that it may be most valuable to readers and support the dreaming community's conversation. And, of course, Denise Linn, who certified me as a Gateway Dreaming™ coach, and who reminded me to anchor my ideas in the important value of the Dream Incubation process.

This list is by no means a complete list, and the references used in this work are a mere select few in an ever-growing repository of clinical work, certainly they are not inclusive of all the researchers whose work has helped to develop current and ongoing dream theories and studies. To those not mentioned here, a thank you for your contribution to the dreaming conversation.

And, a huge thanks to Tabitha Lahr, who designed and typeset this book. It couldn't have happened with your contribution.

# Images

## Chapter 3

"Egyptian Pyramids." Courtesy Wikimedia Commons. https://commons.wikimedia.org/w/index.php?curid=46018

"Four Column Temple Dedicated to Isis." Image by Carole Raddato, courtesy *Wikimedia Commons.* https://commons.wikimedia.org/w/index.php?search=four+column+sanctuary+of+isis&title=Special:MediaSearch&go=Go&type=image

"Palenque 4." Image by Peter Andersen, courtesy *Wikimedia Commons.* https://commons.wikimedia.org/wiki/-File:Palenque_4.jpg

"The Alchemist" by William Fettes Douglas, Public Domain, Courtesy *Wikimedia Commons.* https://commons.wikimedia.org/w/index.php?curid=255727

"Iroquoian Village." Courtesy *Wikimedia Commons.* https://commons.wikimedia.org/wiki/File%3AIroquoian_Village%2C_Ontario%2C_Canada36.JPG

"A Group on Gogo Tribe Dancing." by Imani selemani Nsamila - Own work, CC BY-SA 4.0, Courtesy *Wikimedia Commons.* https://commons.wikimedia.org/w/index.php?curid=54996277

## Chapter 4

"Sleep Spindle and K-Complex." Courtesy *Wikimedia Commons.* https://upload.wikimedia.org/wikipedia/en/a/a8/Stage2sleep.png

## Chapter 5

"Water Under 12.5hz Vibration" by Jordi Torrents - Own work, CC BY-SA 4.0, Courtesy *Wikimedia Commons.* https://commons.wikimedia.org/w/index.php?curid=44870969

"Water Under 11hz Vibration." by Jordi Torrents - Own work, CC BY-SA 4.0, Courtesy *Wikimedia Commons.* https://commons.wikimedia.org/w/index.php?curid=44870968

"Biophoton Symbolic Representation." By Neolexx. Courtesy *Wikimedia Commons.* https://commons.wikimedia.org/wiki/File:TubeTorque.png

## Chapter 7

"Sigmund Freud." Courtesy *Wikimedia Commons.* https://commons.wikimedia.org/wiki/File:Sigmund_Freud_LIFE.jpg

"Carl Jung." Courtesy *Wikimedia Commons.* https://commons.wikimedia.org/wiki/File:CGJung.jpg

"Fritz Perls." Courtesy *Wikimedia Commons.* https://commons.wikimedia.org/wiki/File%3AFritz_Perls.jpg

## Chapter 8

"Medium 9" Courtesy Death to the Stock Photo.

"Circular Cosmetic Container with Lid. Egpt New Kingdom 18th Dynasty." Courtesy *Wikimedia Commons*. https://commons.wikimedia.org/wiki/File%3ACircular_Cosmetic_Container_with_Lid_-_Egypt%2C_New_Kingdom%2C_Dynasty_18%2C_c._1539-1292_BC%2C_ivory_-_Brooklyn_Museum_-_Brooklyn%2C_NY_-_DSC08667.JPG

"Barn owl" by Jean-Jacques Bijou. Courtesy Flickr.com.

Pier image courtesy Keith Misner. Courtesy Death to the Stock Photo.

# Bibliography

Angarita, Gustavo A., Emadi, N., Hodges, S., and Morgan, P. T. (2014). "Sleep Abnormalities Associated with Alcohol, Cannabis, Cocaine, and Opiate Use: A Comprehensive Review." *Addiction Science and Clinical Practice*. Vol 11, No. 9.

Barrett, Dierdre. (1993). "The Committee of Sleep: A Study of Dream Incubation for Problem Solving." *Dreaming*, Vol. 3, No. 2., 115-122.

Beatty, Chester. (1930). "Papyrus." https://www.britishmuseum.org/collection/object/Y_EA10683-3

Bethards, Betty. (1995). *The Dream Book*. Element, Rockport, MA.

Braden, Gregg. (2007). *The Divine Matrix*. Hay House Books, Carlsbad, CA.

Braden, Gregg. (2008). *The Spontaneous Healing of Belief: Shattering the Paradigm of False Limits*. Hay House Books, Carlsbad, CA.

Delaney, Gayle. (1976). "A Proposed Dream Experiment: Phase-Focusing Dream Incubation." *Sundance: Community Dream Journal*, Vol 1., No. 1., 71-83.

Delaney, Gayle. (2015). "Dream Incubation: Targeting Dreaming to Focus on Particular Issues." In M. Kramer & M. Glucksman (Eds.), *Dream research: Contributions to clinical practice* (pp. 38–55). Routledge/Taylor & Francis Group, New York, NY.

Delaney, Gayle. (1996). *Living Your Dreams: The Classic Best Seller on Becoming Your Own Dream Expert*. Harper Collins, New York , NY.

Emoto, Masaru. (2001). *The Hidden Messages in Water.* Atria Books, New York, NY.

Fromm, Erich. (1957). *The Forgotten Language*. Grove Press, New York, NY.

Hall, Calvin S. and Vernon J. Nordby. (1954). *A Primer of Freudian Psychology*. Penguin Books, New York, NY.

Hall, Calvin S. and Vernon J. Nordby. (1973). *A Primer of Jungian Psychology*. Penguin Books, New York, NY.

Hallman, Christian. (2007). "Part One: A Multidimensional Model of the Dreaming State of Consciousness." *Subtle Energies and Energy Medicine*. Vol 18. No. 2., 75.

Heidegger, Martin. (1996). *Being and Time*. State University of New York, Albany, NY.

Hobson, J. Allan, Pace-Schott, E. F., Stickgold, R., Kahn, D. (1998). "To dream or not to dream? Relevant data from new neuroimaging and electrophysiological studies." *Current Opinion in Neurobiology*, Vol. 8, Issue 2.

Hughes, J. Donald. (2000.) "Dream Interpretation in Ancient Civilizations." *Dreaming*, 10(1), 7-18.

Hurd, Ryan. (2015). *Stones, Caves, and Dreams: Digging into the New Transpersonal Psychology*. International Association for the Study of Dreams PsiberDreaming Conference, September 27-Octboer 11, 2015.

Jung, Carl Gustav. (1979). *Aion: Researches into the Phenomenology of the Self. (Collected Works of C. G. Jung, Vol. 9, Part 2)*. Princeton University Press, New York, NY.

Jung, Carl Gustav. (1974). *Dreams*. Princeton University Press. Princeton, NJ.

Jung, Carl Gustav. (1968). *Man and His Symbols*. Dell Publishing, New York, NY.

Jung, Carl Gustav. (1961). *Memories, Dreams, Reflections.* Random House, New York, NY.

Koch, Christof. (June 1, 2018). "What is Consciousness?" *Scientific American.* https://www.scientificamerican.com/article/what-is-consciousness/#

Kompanje, E. J. O. (2008). "'The devil lay upon her and held her down.' Hypnagogic hallucinations and sleep paralysis described by the Dutch physician Isbrand van Diemerbroeck (1609-1674) in 1664." *Journal of Sleep Research,* Vol. 17, No. 4, 464-467.

Krippner, Stanley, Ullman, MD, M., and Vaughn, A. (2003). *Dream Telepathy: Experiments in Nocturnal Extrasensory Perception.* Hampton Roads Publishing Company, Newburyport, MA.

Linn, Denise. (1998). *The Hidden Power of Dreams.* Hay House Books, Carlsbad, CA.

Lipton, Bruce. (2016). *The Biology of Belief.* Hay House Books, Carlsbad, CA.

Lucas, Sabine. (2005). *Past Life Dreamwork.* Bear & Company, Rochester, VT.

Lutz, A., Greischar, L. L., Rawlings, N. B., Ricard, M., & Davidson, R. J. (2004). "Long-term meditators self-induce high-amplitude gamma synchrony during mental practice." *Proceedings of the National Academy of Sciences of the United States of America, 101*(46), 16369–16373. https://doi.org/10.1073/pnas.0407401101.

Lydick, Kelly. "Color in Dreams: the Energy Centers and Their Palette of Greater Meaning." International Association for the Study of Dreams PsiberDreaming Conference, September 27-October 11, 2015.

Mascaro, Kimberly. (2017). *Extraordinary Dreams: Visions, Announcements and Premonitions Across Time and Place.* McFarland & Company Inc. Publishers, Jefferson, NC.

McCleary, Chris. (2015). *Project August: Revolutionary Precognition*. International Association for the Study of Dreams PsiberDreaming Conference, September 27-October 11, 2015.

Moss, Robert. (1996). *Conscious Dreaming: A Spiritual Path for Everyday Life*. Crown Trade Paperbacks, New York, NY.

Moss, Robert. (2005). *Dreamways of the Iroquois: Honoring the Secret Wishes of the Soul*. Destiny Books, Rochester, VT.

Moss, Robert. (2009). *The Secret History of Dreaming*. New World Library, Novato, CA.

Murphy, Joseph. (2008). *The Power of the Subconscious Mind*. Prentice Hall Press, New York, NY.

Nielsen, T., Carr, M., Blanchette-Carrière, C., Marquis, L.-P., Dumel, G., Solomonova, E., . . . Paquette, T. (2017). "NREM sleep spindles are associated with dream recall." *Sleep Spindles & Cortical Up States*, Vol. 1, No. 1, 27–41.

Radin, Dean. (2006). *Entangled Minds*. Paraview Pocket Books, New York, NY.

Reed, Henry. (1976). "Dream Incubation: A Reconstruction of a Ritual in Contemporary Form." *Journal of Humanistic Psychology*. Vol. 16, No. 4, 52-70.

Schoch, Sarah F., Cordi, M. J., Schredl, M., and Rasch, B. (2019). "The Effect of Dream Report Collection and Dream Incorporation on Memory Consolidation During Sleep." *Journal of Sleep Research*. Vol 28. Issue 1.

Siclari, Francesca, Bernardi, G., Cataldi, J. and Tononi, G.. (2018). "Dreaming in NREM Sleep: A High-Density EEG Study of Slow Waves and Spindles." *Journal of Neuroscience*, Vol. 38 No. 43, 9175-9185.

Schopenhauer, Arthur. (2016). *The World as Will and Representation*. Aegitas Digital Publishing, Toronto, Ontario.

Schwitzgebel, Eric. (2002). "Why did we think we dreamed in black and white?" *Studies in History and Philosophy of Science*. No. 33, 649-660.

Sisgold, Steve. (June 4, 2013). "Limited Beliefs." *Psychology Today.* https://www.psychologytoday.com/us/blog/life-in-body/201306/limited-beliefs

Talbot, Michael. (1991). *The Holographic Universe.* Harper Perennial, New York, NY.

Thomas, Julia. (February 2021). "What is the Preconscious and What Does It Mean to Me?" *Betterhelp.com* https://www.betterhelp.com/advice/general/what-is-the-preconscious-and-what-does-it-mean-to-me/

Valderrama, M., Crépon, B., Botella-Soler, V., Martinerie, J., Hasboun, D., Alvarado-Rojas, C., Baulac, M., Adam, C., Navarro, V., & Le Van Quyen, M. (2012). "Human gamma oscillations during slow wave sleep." *Plos One,* 7(4), e33477. https://doi.org/10.1371/journal.pone.0033477

Vedfelt, Ole. (2002). *The Dimensions of Dreams.* Jessica Kingsley Publishers, London, United Kingdom.

Vertes, Robert P. (2004). "Memory Consolidation in Sleep: Dream or Reality?" *Neuron.* Vol 44, Issue 1.

Wohlleben, Peter. (2015). *The Hidden Life of Trees.* Greystone Books, Vancouver, Canada.

Wolf, Fred Allan. (December 1987). "The Physics of Dream Consciousness: Is the Lucid Dream a Parallel Universe?" Second Lucid Dreaming Symposium/Proceedings/Lucidity Letter 6, No. 2.

# About the Author

Kelly Lydick received her Bachelor's degree in Writing & Literature from Burlington College, and her Master's degree in Writing & Consciousness from the New College of California. Her writing has been published in literary and commercial magazines including *Natural Awakenings, Yoga + Life, Guernica, Tarpaulin Sky, Drunken Boat, True Blue Spirit,* and many more. She's also been featured on NPR's *The Writers' Block*, the *Word* podcast, and iHeart radio, among others.

She is the author of *Mastering the Dream* an experimental work about a young woman coming to terms with consciousness. She's also a contributing author to the anthologies *Dreams That Change Our Lives; My Journal, My Journey;* and *Are You the*

*Missing Piece?* She's also a co-founding editor of *Immanence: The Journal of Applied Myth, Story, and Folklore* and founder and owner of The Story Laboratory, a complete publishing consulting firm.

Kelly holds certifications as a Reiki Master, Meditation Facilitator, Crystal Reiki Master, Animal Reiki Master, and in Music Therapy & Sound Healing, and Mindfulness. She also holds certifications as a Life Coach and Gateway Dreaming™ Coach.

She holds professional memberships with the International Association for the Study of Dreams, where she has presented her work on dreams, and the Academy of American Poets.

In 2016, Kelly was honored with a Juno Award for women's leadership from the internationally-renowned Omega Institute of Rhinebeck, New York, for her consulting business Waking the Dream.

In 2019, Kelly was part of the inaugural class of Eckhart Tolle's School of Awakening. She teaches creative writing and personal growth workshops and offers coaching services to individuals, groups, and small and large businesses through her consulting company, Waking the Dream. You can contact her at: www.kellylydick.com.

# Also by Kelly Lydick, M.A.

Kelly Lydick is the author of *Mastering the Dream.*

## *Mastering the Dream*

An experimental work about a young woman coming to terms with what it means to have consciousness. Published by Second Story Books and applauded by literati, this work will change the way you think about the intersections of science and mysticism, and the spiritual and material.

Kelly Lydick is a contributing author to
*Dreams That Change Our Lives.*

## *Dreams That Change Our Lives*
**Robert J. Hoss & Robert P. Gongloff, Editors**

Have you ever awakened from a dream that left you feeling stunned—a dream so vivid or impactful—so unexpected—that it changes your life from that point forward? Imagine you could ask a question of a dream character, or the dream itself, and watch as a profoundly surprising response appears. Suppose you could take action in your dream to eliminate a recurring nightmare, heal a relationship, or even a physical ailment. The 100 dreams in this book have!